Check out all of the books in the Tell Me About Dinosaurs Series

Tell Me About Dinosaurs
ANKYLOSAURUS
xist Publishing

Tell Me About Dinosaurs
BRACHIOSAURUS
xist Publishing

Tell Me About Dinosaurs
SPINOSAURUS
xist Publishing

Tell Me About Dinosaurs
STEGOSAURUS
xist Publishing

Tell Me About Dinosaurs
TRICERATOPS
xist Publishing

Tell Me About Dinosaurs
TYRANNOSAURUS REX
xist Publishing

Tell Me About Dinosaurs
VELOCIRAPTOR
xist Publishing

Published in the United States by Xist Publishing
www.xistpublishing.com

First Edition
Hardcover ISBN: 978-1-5324-5499-8
Paperback ISBN: 978-1-5324-5500-1
eISBN: 978-1-5324-5498-1

PUBLISHED IN TEXAS

Tell Me About Dinosaurs
STEGOSAURUS

Marjorie Seevers

xist Publishing

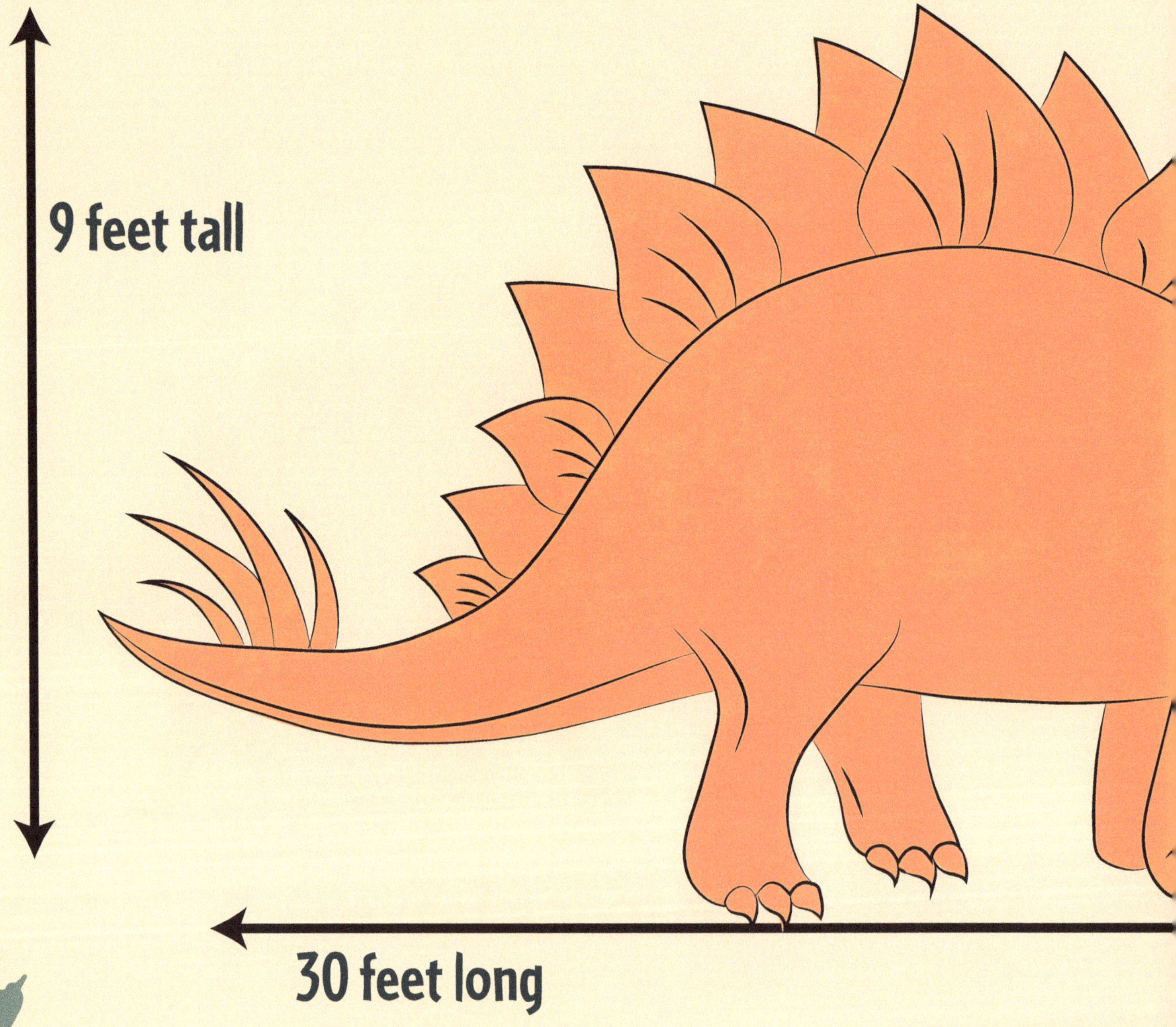
9 feet tall
30 feet long

Stegosaurus was a big dinosaur.

It ate plants.

Stegosaurus had bony plates on its back.

It had spikes on its tail.

Stegosaurus walked on four legs.

It had a small head and a big body.

Stegosaurus bones are called fossils.

Which dinosaur is a Stegosaurus?

What did Stegosaurus eat?

www.ingramcontent.com/pod-product-compliance
Lightning Source LLC
LaVergne TN
LVHW070835080426
835508LV00031B/3482
* 9 7 8 1 5 3 2 4 5 5 0 0 1 *